As the British Empire grew, so too did the scope and range of travel writing. From young men seeking outdoor adventure to intrepid ladies of a certain age discovering other cultures, Victorian explorers were going further and writing more.

But for Lady Colin Campbell—that infamous almost-divorcee with "the unbridled lust of a Messalina and the indelicate readiness of a common harlot"—travel writing was no sterile, fact-driven pursuit. Her adventures up and down European mountains, through unsavoury and unexpected parts of London, by means of delayed train or unstable bicycle, are more than a guidebook. These highly personal travelling tales are the "Trip Advisor" tours of Victorian Britain, the holiday newsletters of the nineteenth century, and the blog posts of another age.

The books in "Found on the Shelves" have been chosen to give a fascinating insight into the treasures that can be found while browsing in The London Library. Now celebrating its 175th anniversary, with over seventeen miles of shelving and more than a million books, The London Library has become an unrivalled archive of the modes, manners and thoughts of each generation which has helped to form it.

From essays on sherry and claret to a passionate defence of early air travel, from advice on how best to navigate the Victorian dinner party to accounts of European adventures, they are as readable and relevant today as they were more than a century ago — even if Louis XV. heels are no longer needed to make it to the other side of Billingsgate Market!

A WOMAN'S WALKS

*Studies in Colour
Abroad and at Home*

The London Library

Pushkin Press

Pushkin Press
71–75 Shelton Street,
London WC2H 9JQ

Chapters selected from Lady Colin Campbell, *A Woman's Walks: Studies
in Colour Abroad and at Home*. With a frontispiece reproduced from a
water-colour portrait by Percy Anderson. London: Eveleigh Nash, 1903

"A Fruit-Stall" by Ettore Tito (1859–1941), published in Henry Perl,
Venezia. London: Sampson Low, Marston & Co., 1894

"Court of the Palazzo Marino" by Ernest C. Peixotto (1869–1940),
published in Edith Wharton, *Italian Backgrounds*. London: Macmillan,
1905

Illustration of a Normandy *curé*, published in George M. Musgrave, *A
Ramble Through Normandy; or, Scenes, Characters and Incidents in a
Sketching Excursion Through Calvados*. London: David Bogue, 1855

"Gold Melting", published in George Frederick Ansell, *The Royal
Mint: its Working, Conduct, and Operations, Fully and Practically
Explained, With Suggestions for its Better Scientific and Official
Management*. London: Effingham Wilson, 1870

"Interior of a Signal-Box", published in John Pendleton, *Our Railways:
Their Origin, Development, Incident and Romance*. London: Cassell
and Co., 1894

First published by Pushkin Press in 2016

9 8 7 6 5 4 3 2 1

ISBN 978 1 782273 23 3

Set in Goudy Modern by Tetragon, London

Printed by CPI Group (UK) Ltd, Croydon, CR0 4YY

www.pushkinpress.com

A WOMAN'S WALKS

BY LADY COLIN CAMPBELL

LADY COLIN CAMPBELL (née Gertrude Elizabeth
Blood), born in 1857, was best known for the divorce
scandal which shocked Victorian society. After four
years of marriage, she sued for divorce on grounds
of her husband's infidelity and cruelty. Lord Colin
alleged that his wife had committed adultery with
at least four men. No divorce was obtained, and she
became a successful writer, editor and journalist, a
member of The London Library, and died in 1911.

Lady Colin Campbell

A Venetian Market

It is not only in the gondola that the charm of Venice is to be felt: the popular notion that there is no walking to be done in the City of the Sea is as fallacious as most popular notions usually are. I know Venice too well to give in to this idea, and so one morning I start off in the clear golden sunlight up the Riva degli Schiavoni, where the first morning *vaporetti* are starting for the Lido and for Chioggia, and the gondoliers are lounging about lazily, knowing that it is yet too early for the *forestieri*, as a rule, to be afoot and afloat. I reach the Piazzetta, and see a friend coming across from the Zecca opposite, but we are both too consistent Venetians to court *malanni* by meeting on the ill-omened space between the pillars of St. Mark and St. Theodore, where the executions were ordered by the Council of Ten to take place, so as to put a stop to the gambling-tables which stood there; so instead we meet and exchange greetings under the loggia, where formerly the Austrian cannon stood ready pointed into the heart of the fair Queen of the Adriatic. My friend is going for a morning constitutional along the Riva to the Giardini Pubblici; I am bound for the market beyond the Rialto; so we part, and I continue my way across the Piazzetta, not forgetting to glance upward at the little shrine of the Madonna, where every evening two tiny lamps are lighted in perpetual memory of the Fornaretto, the young baker who was falsely accused and unjustly executed for a murder he had never committed.

Those birds of prey, the guides, are hardly yet astir, so one escapes their offers of personal guidance, reiterated in that extraordinary *mayonnaise* of languages which is the peculiar *lingua franca* of the tribe in every country; the glorious façade of the most beautiful church in Christendom (at last free from scaffoldings) is bathed in the morning sunshine, which lights up the golden burnish on the great bronze horses, as they stand pawing the air above the doorway. Out here in the sunshine everything is golden, and quiet, and motionless; but as I turn down the Merceria, and penetrate still farther into the heart of the labyrinth, going from one narrow *calle* to the other, crossing a bridge here, passing under a *sotto-portico* there, one seems to get into another world. A world of luminous greys and transparent browns, splashed here and there by wandering rays of sunlight that have lost their way and cannot get back again to the blue sky, of which one has an occasional glimpse overhead; a world no longer silent, majestic, and peaceful, as out there in the silvery Piazza by the sapphire sea, but full of the life and bustle of a Southern crowd intent on its little every-day affairs. The fish ordinaries, as I suppose they would be called in London, are doing a roaring trade; each one crowded with people breakfasting off the innumerable varieties of cooked fish, which lie in large open dishes round the shop, and are ranged in the windows behind wire gratings to attract the passers-by.

I am in no hurry, now that I have got beyond the ordinary tourist haunts, so I wind in and out from one *calle* to another, each one narrower than the last, until I finally come out on the Riva del Carbon by the Grand Canal, and, after stopping to admire the skill and good temper of every one concerned in the disentangling of a huge barge, which has got into a side canal a great deal too small for its bulky proportions, and threatens ruin and destruction to half a dozen gondolas and sandolos, I pass along, and, turning to the left, ascend the steps of the great stone bridge, the Rialto, which was erected by the Doge Pasquale Cicogna in 1588, who therefore adorned it with his crest, a stork or *cicogna*, in allusion to his family name.

Verily it is a motley crowd that is passing up and down between the lines of small shops that divide the width of the great bridge into three thoroughfares.

The women clatter along in their fascinating wooden *zoccoli*, which are so becoming to the feet when the wearer is young and carries herself erect; when the wearer is old and bent, and the heels protude at the back beyond the wooden sole, then the effect is perhaps not so happy. Their heads and figures are draped in the long pointed shawls of every imaginable colour, for here we are among the *popolo*, and the smart black mantillas of the *bourgeoisie* are unknown except, perhaps, on *festa* days. Here and there I see a woman from the mainland of Lombardy, her head flashing with a nimbus of large silver pins thrust in a semicircle into the plaits at the back of her head. The little children toddle along, clattering also in their *sciabatte*, holding on to a corner of the mother's shawl, or else the little one is nestling on its mother's arm, and the one shawl covers the two dark heads and the wondering brown eyes, and every woman and child is thus transformed into a Madonna and Bambino. One wonders no more that the painters of old never wearied of painting such a subject, when it was daily suggested to them by such models.

Wandering merchants are many on the great bridge, and I have my choice of breaking my fast on small cuttlefish—crimson and knotty abominations, which the vendor lifts on a stick for my benefit out of a beautiful old copper basin—roasted pumpkins in glorious slices of orange and green, or *pan-forte di Siena*, a compound of burnt almonds and hazelnuts, toothsome but unwholesome. Being fortunately possessed of the digestion of an ostrich, and having fond memories of the esteem with which I regarded *pan-forte* when a child, I decide in favour of the latter, and descend into the market, munching serenely.

The market is aglow with life and colour. I stop at a poultry-stall, where the chickens are trussed in a comical way, with their heads looking out from under the pinion of one wing: it is not chickens I sigh over, however, but the bunches of little birds of all sorts—blackcaps, chaffinches, thrushes, and, alas! redbreasts too, that are hung up for sale. Underneath are the trays of *beccafichi*, their little bare red bodies looking, at a distance, like red sea-anemones. They are not half the size of the little green figs they are said to live upon, which are to be found at the next stall, where a riot of grapes, black and golden, is being poured out from the baskets which have just arrived. The bloom is still on them like hoar-frost, so I plunge in behind the stall among the baskets, and am lost to sight for many minutes, after which I emerge rather sugary about the finger-tips, having sampled all the grapes—the curiously-flavoured black *fragole* as well as the greenish *moscata*, and the sweet, juicy vineyard grapes that taste of the sun; and bearing a bulgy paper parcel, that threatens to "come undone," as the children say, in a most distressing manner at every step. However, this is but the first of many parcels, for who that is fructivorous could refrain from buying in the midst of such profusion? Figs, tender, green, and luscious, each bearing testimony to its internal excellence by the little drop of gum which adorns one end, follow next, and then pears of all sizes and colours, from the big Jerseys to the tiny red "Canadas," until we finally can carry no more, and on counting up, find we have expended the enormous sum of a franc and a half!

A Fruit-Stall

Laden like the spies from Canaan, and like them laden with fruit, we leave the market-place and, picking our steps amongst heaps of huge pumpkins, grey-green, olive, red, and orange in colour, that might serve, any one of them, for the chariot of Cinderella, we make our way to the Pesceria, or fish-market. We pass a woman sitting, like the figure of Titian's mother in the picture of the "Presentation of the Virgin," between a basket of eggs and another of live doves, whose pure white plumage would seem to mark them out for sacrifice. The cast-iron roofing to the fish-market is a new institution, far from ornamental to the Grand Canal, but no doubt useful to the vendors who have their stalls beneath. Never have I seen such a wonderful variety of sea-beasts disposed for sale. Fish of all shapes and sizes, to which I do not even attempt to give names: some striped like tigers, others spotted like the pard; red fish, white fish, green fish, blue fish, fish that are all body and no head, fish that are all head and no body. In size there is the same variety: at one end of the scale is whitebait, at the other a gigantic tunny which is being cut into slices that look just like steaks of horseflesh, while in between are small sharks, evil-looking beasts even in death. "Eels a many" are wallowing in buckets and tubs, sticky, slimy masses of dark olive-green, flanked by crawling heaps of tiny, gruesome-looking crabs and jumping masses of large greyish-brown *gamberi* or shrimps, awaiting the cauldron which is to improve their complexions and turn them a rosy red. In and about all these *frutta di mare* are strange-looking piles, some snow-white, others steel-grey, others again white and grey, and all garnished with dreadful eyes that follow one with a glassy stare. With a shudder I discover that they are various kinds of sepias and octopods, which the omniverous Venetians look upon as toothsome and delicious morsels. One merchant presses upon me a dish of these revolting creatures ready prepared for cooking, cut into long strips that suggest macaroni; and as I look at them askance, I secretly wonder how near death by starvation would have to come before I would consent to make such a gastronomic experiment.

The mere thought of eating one of those dreadful things with their glassy eyes makes one feel cold all over; so we flee back to the Rialto, where we only pause to purchase a poor little live bird that some children of Belial (is it necessary to particularise that they were small boys?) have captured and are worrying after the manner of their kind; and then we plunge once more into the twilight of the *calle*, where the red and green peppers, and the piles of fruit and vegetables at the stalls, make blots of colour in dark places, and so return to the Piazza. Here we let go our captive bird; but it is too tired and bewildered to fly more than a few yards, when, with a cry of glee, it is captured by a *facchino*, who proceeds to carry it off in triumph. But it is not for that I released the prisoner from the boys, so I start off in pursuit, and, in vigorous Venetian, denounce the pirate and reclaim my property. There is some danger to the victim of the dispute, as the pirate is loth and indignant; but I am not to be daunted, and having made good my claim, I carry off the frightened birdling to the steps of the Luna, and bribe a gondolier to take it across to the Royal Gardens, where it finally regains its liberty among the trees and flowers. And thus feeling that my morning walk has at least benefited one living thing besides myself, I return happy and hungry to my temporary home.

Marooned at Milan

For the collecting of varied experience there is nothing like being a good-natured idiot. A reluctance to say "No" to unreasonable requests, especially from helpless brother or sister idiots, is apt to introduce all sorts of variations into the quietest and best-ordered existence. This is no doubt the reward; for who would sooner "rest unburnished" rather than "shine in us"? When, therefore, a friend of mine in the same hotel, and undergoing the same admirable cure at Salsomaggiore, received bad news about a little child she is devotedly attached to, and determined to start for England by the same evening's train, what could I do but say, "Why, certainly!" when she implored me to take her to Milan and see her into the express, as she neither knows nor understands a single word of Italian? A prolonged study of the mysteries of the "orario," with its bewildering method of counting by twenty-four hours instead of twelve, and its habit of requiring often to be read up the column instead of down (this being indicated by arrows pointing upwards), at last reveals the fact that by starting at nineteen o'clock we can reach Milan at twenty-two o'clock, and having carefully deposited my friend in the through Calais express, I can myself take the forty minutes past twenty-two, and return to the little wayside station of Borgo San Donnino soon after the understandable hour of midnight. Having wrenched this fact from the Sibylline leaves of the "orario," I toss it on the table with an "Ouf!" of relief, and look no further, but order the carriage to meet me at midnight at the station, three-quarters of an hour's drive from Salsomaggiore.

The little steam-tram crawls away with us down the valley, and after having leant against four or five farmhouses by the roadside (which are dignified by placards, just as if they were real stations), finally shrieks its way into Borgo San Donnino through the narrow streets, almost grazing the houses, and pulls up with a series of exhausted jerks at the station. Having done this, it drags itself back to Salsomaggiore, and rests from its labours through the night. We enter the diminutive station, have our tickets closely and sus-piciously examined by the guardian angel in buttons who watches at the door of that dusty paradise the waiting-room, and prepare to await the Roman express, which will graciously allow us to board it on its road to Milan.

We wait a quarter of an hour; half an hour; an hour; and still no train appears. We wrap ourselves in our cloaks, without which no wise people in Italy venture forth at or after sundown; we curse silently, and encourage our fellow victims to curse as openly as their command of language will admit. Whenever the red-capped station-master ventures out of hiding, we all rush at him with vociferous questions; whereupon he shrugs his shoulders, spreads out his arms, ejaculates "Ma!" and vanishes. At last, after a delay of an hour and a half, the train (which had all but had a serious accident near Florence) arrives full of dusty, tired, and furious passengers; we are all tumbled in somehow, and off we go across the flat plain of Lombardy, over the Po, with the bridge of boats etched in black across the surface of the great river glittering in the moonlight; and then through the thick white mists of the best-irrigated and most fertile country in Europe, where the hay is mown twelve times a year, and mulberry, maize, and vine make the whole country look like a garden. The wreaths of mist are fantastically beautiful as they rise with the wind of our passage from the willows and acacias that border the line; but it is no use pointing them out to my poor friend, for her whole mind is fixed on the problem of whether the through express will await the arrival of this one or not. I am careful not to express my own conviction that it will not; but the Romans in the carriage, with all their sense of the importance of the express coming from the capital city, unanimously declare that it is impossible it should not wait. They know their railways better than I, for, in spite of our being eighty minutes late on reaching Milan, the express is still there, snorting with indignation. There is just time to rush over level-crossings, regardless of locomotives sliding to and fro, find a place for my friend and her belongings, and off they go!

The *facchino* who has carried the impedimenta turns to me with a smile of triumph, as if our having caught the train by the tail, as it were, was entirely owing to him. When I ask when the next train starts for Borgo San Donnino, I regret to say that the smile becomes a grin. "The last train left an hour ago," he remarks cheerfully in his best Milanese; "you must have passed it on the road." We did; and it suddenly bursts upon me that I am marooned at Milan at midnight, without even the limited resources of a hand-bag to depend upon! And here I must make a confession in the interests of veracity. I *ought*, by all the rules that should govern the mind of a sensitive, proper-minded female, to be overcome with dismay at finding myself friendless, soap-less, comb-less, curling-tong-less, alone and unprotected in a strange city "as the clocks are chiming the hour" of midnight! But I am *not*; or rather, when I realise the entire novelty of the situation, I am so overcome with a sense of exhilaration at being for once in my life absolutely *free*, with no more responsibility than a bird on the wing, that I very nearly dance a riga-doon of delight on the dusty metals of the line before an advancing engine!

I give up my ticket to the collector with a friendly "*Ciaò!*" that but feebly expresses my amiability towards an all-wise railway company that has provided me with so novel an experience, and then I am out of the station, out where the great arc-lights are deepening the purple night-sky, and making the stars shrink backward before their blatant self-assertiveness. What a sky for the roof of the Hotel of the Beautiful Star! and why should I not for once gratify my primitive nomadic instincts, which are bubbling strong in me to-night, and eschew four walls altogether? I think of the bastions with their stone benches under the spreading horse-chestnuts that are so intoxicating a glory in the spring. One might do worse than spend a night there playing hide-and-seek with the stars through the great branches—

"Près des remparts de Seville,
    Chez mon ami, Lillas Pastia,"

I hum to myself as I stand looking up at the sky, filled to overflowing with the joy of liberty, and swaying to the lilt of the seguidilla. Nobody knows where I am; nobody (here in Milan) cares what I do. But, alas! that blissful notion pulls me up with a round turn, as the sailors say, and my thoughts fly off at a tangent to the little village among the foothills of the Apennines, where kindly hearts enclosed in kindly bodies are keeping vigil anxiously for my promised return. Those kindly hearts have fervid imaginations, and will soon be imagining every kind of dire happening and disaster befalling me when I do not return; so the least I can do is to minimise picturesque possibilities and go quietly to an hotel.

However, the sacrifice of the Hotel of the Beautiful Star and of the bastions has its reward; for my sense of humour is vastly tickled by the expression of the proprietor of the hotel when I drive up in the omnibus I have commandeered from the station. A strange female, speaking Italian with a distinct Florentine accent (so my Neapolitan friends tell me), who arrives after midnight without an atom of luggage, and gives an English name, is a combination calculated to "knock the stuffing" out of the average hotel-keeper. It clearly does; so having sailed into the hotel and taken possession by right of conquest, I restore mine host's scattered wits and equanimity by giving the magic name of the friend who had recommended me to go to this hotel if I should be in Milan; and I also explain the heart-rending facts of the missed train. Thereafter smiles and hot soup are my portion; and the "povera signora" is hoisted up in a lift (there would have been no need for lifts on the bastions!) and conducted into a room all velvet furniture and gilding, gigantic mirrors, and slippery floor. I feel inclined to upset the furniture and break the mirrors as soon as I am shut into this gilded cage after my fleeting glimpse of freedom; but the sight and touch of the snowy linen sheets console me, and humming the seguidilla I am soon lost in the Land of Dreams...

I am awakened by the connubial warblings of an

unmistakably American couple in the next room. Dear me! what strange forms of expression Yankee matrimony takes upon itself in privacy, or at least what it is pleased to suppose is privacy! I carefully examined and locked all the four doors of my stately apartment on taking possession, and my arrival last night as well as my movements this morning must have informed my neighbours of my presence; but it makes no difference, and they continue to exchange remarks partly candid, partly cryptic, to my exceeding amusement. A bath is a poor thing when shorn of sponge, soap, and perfumes; and my tramp's toilette is not a lengthy business, nor my breakfast either. As there is no train for several hours, I salve my conscience for feeling so exhilarated by sending off a telegram explaining the mishap, and announcing my return; and then, calling a *carrozella*, am off into the fresh morning air and sunshine, up the beautiful Corso Venezia, the palaces on either hand affording glimpses, through their entrances,

Court of the Palazzo Marino

of pillared courtyards and lovely gardens full of palms and flowers. Milan is a most beautiful city; her one and only drawback being the cobble-stones with which she paves her streets. The little electric trams go sliding and tinkling their way up and down all the main streets; and I almost regret I did not prefer their smoothness to the jolting of the *carrozella*, drawn by a white horse with an inordinately long tail, which it flourishes wildly every time it is admonished by its very ancient and somewhat irritable master. First we go to the Duomo, to renew—who shall say how many?—memories with that beautifully spacious interior, where the services can go on in due order in the raised sanctuary, and the rest of the church is left gloriously empty for the repose of mind of the dreaming wanderer.

Mass is being said at the high altar by a bishop whose mitre shines from afar, even through the clouds of incense and the twilight of the sanctuary. Above the altar a great crimson drapery, hanging from a golden crown, is drawn out in wings at either side; it symbolises, as it were, the shelter that the Church would offer to all—like the hen "gathering her chickens under her wings." Above the entrance to the sanctuary, high up in the point of the arch, hangs a colossal golden crucifix in mid-air, the light from the upper clerestory windows falling on it, and making it stand out with curious vividness against the mysterious background of twilit shadows; and underneath it, on an invisible wire, pulsates a solitary star-like lamp, a light that is never quenched night or day. People are passing to and fro continually: workmen on their way to work, who enter for a moment into the Home of Peace, that is open to all; graceful Milanese women and damsels, their comely heads set off with the ever-charming black veils, which also adorn the fair curly heads of the tiny girls who toddle at their sides, trying to combine the necessity of holding on to their mothers' skirts with the task of pulling up the mittens that cover their little fat brown paws; *forestieri* by the dozen, Germans and Americans chiefly, their appearance being sufficient to announce their nationality, even without the unmistakable red-covered Baedeker peeping out of pockets or from under arms; occasionally that most terrible double-headed monster, a German bride and bridegroom, who even in church walk arm-in-arm with an amount of loving demonstration that makes one long for the days of Carrier and *les noyades*, that one might drown them at once and together, to be sure of getting rid of both.

Perhaps it is the spectacle of an unusually aggressive pair that first fills my mind with murderous desires, and then, not unnaturally, turns my thoughts to methods of interment; for an idea occurs to me of a profitable experience to be made, and, leaving the cool asylum of the Duomo, I re-enter the *carrozella* and request to be taken to the cemetery. It is not a long drive, and we soon pass beyond the walls and pull up before the gates of a great black-and-white building that encloses three sides of a courtyard. The building consists of a line of colonnades connecting various temples or pavilions, raised upon a low basement storey also pierced with arches, through which one walks into the vast cemetery that stretches beyond. White and green on every side—the white of marble, the green of acacia trees—baking under the brilliant sunlight, blind the eyes at every turn. A few people are moving about among the tombs; but the monuments are so many and so big that one soon loses sight of any one, and through a great silence and solitude I pass down the avenues of this City of the Dead, noting on every side the proofs which one finds in foreign cemeteries of the tender affection and remembrance the living bear to those who have gone before into the Silent Land, but which are so grievously conspicuous by their absence from most English burial-grounds. Many of the family vaults are hideous and almost grotesque, the terribly redundant realism that is the bane of modern Italian statuary being responsible for the life-sized statues of children with every detail and accessory of their best "Sunday-go-to-meeting" clothes accurately reproduced; though, indeed, one is disposed to forgive this sumptuary realism when one comes across a tomb such as that of a certain Giulio Rossi, whereon is seated a life-sized figure of a comely, bald-headed old gentleman, who has gone to the other extreme, and is habited solely in a beard! But, on the other hand, some of the vaults are massive, simple structures, full of the solemn dignity of outline that is a fitting frame to "the lordly repose of the dead."

I do not pause long in this part of the Necropolis, for I have a goal in view, which presently comes in sight—a long, single-storey building like a Grecian temple, situated at the far end of the cemetery. Tall marble urns stand at either side of the entrance, at the top of the flight of steps, and others are ranged between the pillars of the façade; for this classic temple is the most famous Milanese crematorium, which has done more to establish cremation than any other building of the kind in the world. Passing up the steps I enter a cool, dark, marble-lined antechamber, wherein sits an official who is amiability itself when I explain I want to see the crematorium. He leads me past an immense sarcophagus, which I afterwards learn is the Chamber of Purifying Fire, and, passing a curtained aperture, shows me the whitewashed car on which the body is placed; it is simply a few bars of iron raised about a foot above a white-metal tray. There is a pall-like cover resting on the ground close by, which is used to cover the body, if desired, until it is introduced into the fire-chamber. Drawing aside the curtain I find myself in a large lofty room, panelled with marble. In one of the walls are two openings, or, rather, two of the slabs of marble slide back to allow one to see into the furnaces, of which there are two, the first one being for cremation by gas-flames, the second for cremation by wood-fire. The gas-flames are far the quicker method, for the chamber is already considerably heated when the body is introduced, and complete incineration is accomplished in fifty minutes; with the wood-fire, the same result is not arrived at under two hours.

I had always understood that cremation was done by sheer heat, and not by actual contact with the flame; but I was wrong, and the Divine Element itself takes the corpse into its all-purifying embrace, and wraps it round in a glorious mantle of flame. What could be more beautiful than the thought of the dead body, introduced into that marble chamber, lying there while the Goddess of Fire descends upon him, and makes him her own, erasing all the impurities of the flesh, wiping out physical defects, blotting out imperfections, and gradually absorbing him into herself, until he becomes one with her godhead, and they depart together, leaving behind nothing but a handful of pure white, coral-like residue, fit symbol of the Great Purification? It is a vision that robs death of its sting and the grave of its unspeakable horrors, of which one cannot think without a shudder. Merciful to the living and the dead, the Goddess of Fire leaves no foulness behind to poison unborn generations, and to mar the holy memory of our loved ones with mental nightmares of bodily corruption; and the only wonder is that the obvious lesson of purity and health should have taken so long to learn, and should even yet be accepted only by the few. I have visited many graveyards, but always with horror and reluctance, as my mind persistently dwelt upon and realised the unspeakable abominations of physical corruption. Besides, the idea of being hidden in a hole in the ground, away from the light and heat of the sun, has always oppressed me like an evil dream; but as I leave the crematorium of Milan I am conscious of nothing but a radiant vision——a chariot of flame to close my earthly record, like that of Elijah——and as I turn to take a last look at the Grecian temple, Chaucer's words come back to me like a prophetic benediction:

"This is the Port of Rest from Troublous Toyle."

The Eternal Hills

The absurd little locomotive which looks like a kneeling camel has pushed the car up the mountain from Glion, and now rests puffing and snorting, and emitting sparks and vile sulphurous smoke, while we of the Caux contingent with difficulty find places aboard. This is not much wonder, for on so glorious a day of baking sunshine and pure fresh air the eternal hills call to every one in a voice not to be denied; and the train to the Rochers de Naye, far above our heads, is consequently packed. As we climb up, with many protesting snorts from the camel in the rear, I realise that Caux is a mountain by itself, a mountain of rock covered with green velvet herbage and pine forests, that divides two deep gorges. In the one lies Les Avants in its sun-trap of verdure far below; above the other rises the rocky bastion of the Rochers de Naye, over six thousand feet above the level of the sea. The line of the mountain railway lies along the steep and grassy ridge which connects the hill of Caux with the great Dent de Jaman, a hoary snag of rock which tops the divide that separates the lovely Corniche of the Lake of Geneva from the deep, broad valley of Gruyère and its mountains beyond.

We pass through a tunnel at the base of the Tooth of Jaman, and curve round to the right along the lip of a deep valley full of the rocky *débris* which has fallen from the precipitous wall of the Rochers de Naye at the opposite side. Among the rocks at the bottom tiny pine-trees are struggling for existence. They have but little in common with the stately armies that climb the hills up which we have travelled, and in this mountain hollow, where the snows stay longer than the sun, the struggle for existence has warped and wizened them into the likeness of Japanese dwarf-trees, among which the browsing cattle look colossal.

At Jaman we stop, to give the locomotive a rest, and to allow those who intend to climb the conical rock to descend from the train. We have left the fertile meadows, sweet with new-mown hay, far behind at the other side of the tunnel; up here the rich, thick pasture is starred with flowers, even though it is no longer the blossoming-time of the Alpine roses, whose bushes mingle with those of the whortleberries along the sides of this mountain combe. Tall yellow asphodels, bronze-coloured giant gentians, masses of bluest mountain forget-me-nots, tiny, deep blue gentians, yellow and purple clover, pink cranesbill, and splendid blue and silver thistles meet the eye at every turn, while the fragrance of wild thyme comes to one in every breath. The bees seem to be quite well aware of the reputation of this mountain-hollow for flowers, and they are busy getting thoroughly and conscientiously drunk (on strictly utilitarian principles) on every side. It is blazing hot at Jaman, where there is no shade larger than that afforded by a thistle; and there is one general sigh of relief when the train moves forward again round the curve of the hollow, and enters the tunnel under the Rochers de Naye.

It is a long tunnel, and as black as Erebus, for the economy of the railway company does not permit lights; and when we once more emerge into the sunshine we feel like moles coming out into an upper world. The hotel stands above us; and another curved tunnel brings us out at the platform just beneath the terrace of the hotel, which is already crowded with visitors brought up by previous trains. We all tumble out of the cars, and while some start to climb the steep rampart of sun-burnt grass, which the grazing cattle have worn into lines like the ripples of sand on a sea-shore, up to the highest point or "Signal" of the Rochers de Naye, I content myself with a bench placed on the edge of the rocks to the south beyond the hotel.

The beauty of the view before me is extraordinary. The rocky bastion on which I am sitting drops sheer to where the grassy, precipitous slopes begin; then come the forests of pines, dipping down out of sight into the depths of the gorge, and rising again on the further side to a serrated line of rocks, from which spring, like two huge antediluvian monster molars, two rocks, La Tour d'Ay and La Tour de Mayen. Away beyond them, and beyond the Valley of the Rhone—of which one gets a glimpse at the foot of the gorge far below—rises the Dent du Midi, over whose shoulder peeps the great giant of all, Mont Blanc himself—a mass of glistening snow in the blue southern sky. He forms the culminating point of that wonderful amphitheatre of eternal snows, which curves away from him by the Aiguille Verte, the Grand Combin (next neighbour to the Great St. Bernard), the Diablerets, the Wildhorn, Balmhorn, Doldenhorn, Blümlisalp, and ends up with that magnificent quartette of peaks, the Jungfrau, Mönch, Eiger, and Wetterhorn away to the north. It is impossible to imagine anything more beautiful or more impressive than this marvellous chain of snow and ice—the realm of the Ice-Queen, who defies Phoebus Apollo, as well as mere mortal man, to make any impression upon her rare and glistening purity; and as one gazes at them, hypnotised by their beauty, one feels more than ever the ineffable loveliness of the world and the indescribable littleness of the human race that bustle over its surface, like the ants over one of the ant heaps in the pine forests at one's feet.

The air up at this height is extraordinarily pure and soft and fresh. It comes sighing up the mountain-side, setting the grasses quivering and the blue aconites and golden Shirley poppies nodding in the flower-beds on the terrace; and it fills one with a delicious spiritual intoxication that seems to put all trouble and sorrow far away out of reach. Great black crows swoop out from the rocks and soar into space, the sun glinting on their blue-black wings, satiny as a woman's hair; and one's thoughts float out into space after them, knowing no bounds, and soar away over those wonderful hills of palest orchid mauve and faintest blue, through the golden haze of sunshine, until everything that is far away seems near, and everything that is near seems far away, and all the world is a dream of perfect peace and loveliness.

The moment is too perfect, however, to last; and one's dreams are rudely dispelled by loud exclamations of "Prachtvoll! Ganz colossal!" as a party of German alpinists arrive on the scene. They are weird beings, grotesquely habited, and quite unnecessarily fat and ugly; and the women seem even more careless of their appearance than the men—if, indeed, one can honour by the name of women creatures of such apparently indeterminate sex. Like the great Napoleon, *je n'aime que les sexes prononçés*; and these fat female Teutons, with red, perspiring faces, surrounded by straggling wisps of sandy hair, clothed in men's shirts and boots and much-abbreviated skirts hitched up with straps round their middles (one could not give the name of waist to such equatorial lines!) and their Falstaffian companions, entirely spoil the beauty of the scene for me. They even frighten the soaring crows, who, with chuckling squawks, swoop off to their homes in the cliffs; so I follow this wise example, and return to the terrace of the hotel, where tea and the inevitable post-cards await us.

I struggled for long against the "postcard habit"; but it is as insidious as other vices, and the Swiss postcards are too pretty to be resisted. So I have fallen as others have done; and with the usual thoroughness of an active mind, have become a very bad case indeed; and I take my walks abroad armed with a stylograph and stamps, punctuating my path through the world by the sending of coloured pictures. However, there are more harmful forms of lunacy, and this mild madness often gives point to an excursion and occupation for many a spare half-hour. It is certainly general, for every table on the crowded terrace is occupied by people of both sexes scribbling frantically; and the postcard stall and post-office do a roaring trade before the train backs up the platform and a rush is made for the preferred corner seats. We are not lucky, or else we possess some unknown and undesired attraction for fat Germans; for four of the fattest specimens tumble into our compartment (there are no separate classes on these democratic mountain railways), and, hailing a waiter for wine, continue to drink till the train starts. There is no room elsewhere, and it is the last train; so there is nothing to be done but to freeze stiff and endure. Jokes born of wine nearly produce apoplexy in my opposite neighbour, an individual whose face might be taken for that of "The Man in the Moon"; when, mercifully, one of the four starts humming a tune, another produces a well-thumbed book of *Volks-Lieder* out of his pocket, and the four launch into part-songs with undeniably sweet voices, which is a distinct improvement on their guttural conversation and loud guffaws. In another country such types of fat tipsters would sing music-hall ditties of doubtful quality under similar circumstances; these instead plunge into impassioned verses addressed to the mountains and the flowers, with occasional excursions into the purely sentimental regions inhabited by *Mädchen*. They continue to warble softly and pleasantly, like four fat red bullfinches; and the blue gooseberry eyes of my opposite neighbour are full of tears as he ecstatically sings what will happen "Wenn ich komm, wenn ich komm, wenn ich wieder um komm" (his vision will probably materialise into chastisement with a broomstick by the wife of his bosom if he returns to her in his present condition!) as we draw up at Caux, and leave the bullfinches to warble alone.

I am in time for the sunset when I reach my balcony, and there leaning out over a depth of two thousand feet, I watch the great inland sea below turn from shimmering blue to orange streaked with mother-of-pearl. Along the horizon lies the purple band of the Jura mountains, behind which the sun is sinking in a ball of molten gold which makes a path across the lake, dividing the orange and pearl and sapphire. The line of the coast with its many indentations, its villas and gardens and nestling white towns, slips away to meet the horizon, and the vine-clad hills glide down to the water,

> "Where tides of grass break into foam of flowers,
> Or where the wind's feet shine along the sea."

The feet of the evening breeze are in truth dappling the water, and making it shine like silver, though the wind is hardly strong enough to fill the lateen sails, set wing-and-wing, of the fishing-boats which float snow-white in this ever-changing sea of colour.

The sun sinks out of sight behind the hills in the wonderful silence of sunset, when the Earth seems to be holding her breath in rapture; and then, round the corner of the mountains opposite, swings into view the slim crescent of the new moon, upright as Diana herself, her delicate line of silver relieved against the crimson and orange, the purple and emerald and gold and sapphire—the final blaze of triumph of the departing sun-god. The sky is still alight in the west when darkness closes down on the great expanse of water; the last sea-gull has gone to rest on its quiet-heaving breast, and, as the darkness climbs higher, the fires in the west pale to turquoise and then deepen to purple. The stars come out overhead; the coast-line becomes Sindbad's Valley of Diamonds, with the lights of all the invisible towns and villas along the lips of the lake, apparently floating in darkness—

"With stars and night-winds in her garments
   Night sinks on the sea";

and as the evening breeze flutters like a sigh up to my balcony, I realise that never in all my wanderings have I seen a more beautiful spot than this mountain eyrie of Caux.

Ixiona

A brilliant, beautiful, blue day. A sea of turquoise, flecked with shadows of amethyst and emerald, and here and there sparkling with white foam-crests, as the breeze that is sending the light fleecy clouds scudding across the sky, just catches the little waves that give life and movement to the great expanse of water, and sends them racing, one after the other, to break on the shingly beach with a lovely silky, rustling cadence of never-ending music. On the wide green lawns that meet the shingle children are playing, while old ladies and quiet nursemaids sit on benches or on heaps of stones and read, knit and gossip, as seemeth best in their eyes. In a quiet corner by the little fort that mounts guard over the harbour a middle-aged *curé* paces slowly along, reading his breviary, his eyes from time to time resting with gentle complacency on the peaceful scene before him, while his lips murmur the well-known words it is his duty to repeat daily. Everything betokens quietness, ruminant existence, absence of emotion of any kind. Alas! that in this imperfect world such things endure but for a time; for, behold! into the heart of this blue-and-white peace comes suddenly Destruction on a bicycle! It is true that Destruction is not having a very happy time of it. It is the first time she has ventured to entrust her precious person to a wobbly wheel, and it is only by main force that the diminutive Frenchman who has taken upon himself to instruct her in the noble art of Ixion maintains her and the vehicle in somewhat of an erect position.

The worst catastrophes in Nature are invariably caused by more or less unconscious agents. An avalanche that begins with a few pebbles rolling down a mountain-side can hardly be credited with the knowledge that it will ultimately obliterate the village in the valley, many hundred feet below; and the innocence of Destruction as to the effects she is likely to produce makes her all the more dangerous. Death himself on the White Horse (not the Rosmer breed of animal!) would hardly cause the same dismay as this black-headed Pestilence riding by noonday on a wheel. The children pause in their play, and seek safety on the centre of the grass-plots; the old ladies' needles are raised from their eternal *tapisserie*, while the *bonnes* who have gravitated towards the four *douaniers* lolling under the wall of the fort cease their flirtations for a moment, and seek shelter behind their admirers. "*Voyons! un bon coup de jarret*" cries the panting and perspiring instructor; while a fly, sent straight by Satan from the Bottomless Pit, settles on his nose. "*La! ça y est!*" and so it is; for what with the increase of speed, the presence of that maddening fly, which the unfortunate teacher cannot brush away (both hands being occupied with his pupil and the bicycle), a big flint under the wheel, or that inherent cussedness of inanimate things which can always be depended on to produce calamities, the bicycle lurches violently to port. There is a short, sharp struggle, a wobble as if the front wheel of the machine were trying to turn round and attack its brother behind, violent efforts on the part of the teacher to maintain the general equilibrium, and then a collapse of everything—pupil, bicycle, and teacher together in a heap at the very feet of the *curé*. The holy man is so overcome at the fluttering and fleeting vision that is given him of pale blue silk and white lace that

he grows violently red, crosses himself hurriedly, and departs with hastening strides to seek some secluded spot where wheels and petticoats cannot pursue him. "*Quand je vous le disais, moi, que je me flanquerais par terre en allant si vîte!*" says Destruction, with very pink cheeks and dangerously black eyes, as she disentangles herself and her skirts from the malignant machine, and proceeds to dust herself vigorously. The little Frenchman sighs, and rubs a considerably damaged elbow. "*Cela ne m'est jamais arrivé,*" he murmurs apologetically, "*mais Madame est si... si belle femme que je ne pouvais pas la maintenir*"—a delightfully euphuistic manner of accounting for the fact that "Madame's" weight had dragged him off his poor little legs which no one but a Frenchman would have thought of. It apparently mollifies the lady, who remounts the offending machine, and the lesson begins again at a more sober pace.

Not once, but many times a day, are similar delightful scenes enacted on the beautiful, spacious *plages* of Normandy; and one certainly requires a special costume, fitted for what might be termed "the requirements of the Fall," when one essays to vanquish the inherent malignity that lurks in that seemingly innocent tandem of wheels. No one knows what original sin means until he or she has studied the true inwardness of a bicycle. I have wrestled for its conversion to the straight path with the fervour of a Salvationist captain at the "Penitents' Bench." The straight path is the one thing the bicycle, until properly broken in and tamed, abhors. It will accommodate you with figures of 8, it will oblige you with the "outside edge" when an omnibus is passing by—I believe it would even "cut a Mohawk" or a "grapevine," if it could get within measurable distance of a passing train, so as to accomplish your final destruction—but until it is fairly conquered it will not go straight. Even after you think you have reduced it to submission, and have eliminated its natural desire for "reeling, writhing, and fainting in coils," by mercilessly sending it along at full speed, a moment's distraction on your part, a passing acquaintance, a gossamer thread floating out from the hedge and tickling your ear, suffices for the ever-watchful demon, who promptly takes the opportunity of swerving violently and depositing you on a heap of stones at the roadside— for heaps of stones are the joy of the bicycle in its unregenerate stage. Dogged determination not to be beaten, however, makes victory but a question of time, and, once conquered, the bicycle becomes a friend, an ally to be depended upon at all times and seasons, an endless delight. To it one owes not only the feeling of absolute independence, of self-sufficiency in the truest and best sense of that much ill-used term, but the knowledge of the sensation of flying. To what else can one compare one's feelings when skimming as lightly and silently as a goat-sucker down a twilit country lane? The pneumatic tyres slip noiselessly over the smooth road, one's feet rise and fall on the pedals so mechanically that one is unconscious of the smallest effort or intention of movement. The grasshoppers chirp in the fields after the heat of the day has passed; in the stillness of the coming night the lowing of the cows being milked on the pasturages in the valley sounds strangely impressive and weird; the bats wheel close overhead, hawking for insects, and uttering their strange mordant cry, that somehow always suggests some sharp cutting instrument of steel; a dog springs barking up at a cottage-gate as one shoots past, more than half his anger arising from the fact that he had not heard one coming, and that his self-conceit as a watchdog has suffered injury.

Under the shadow of the woods one flits along among the varied voices of the unseen creatures of the twilight; while on the high, sloping bank the columns of the beech-trees rise aloft, far overhead, with their magnificent air of splendid virility, and down below the leaves of the aspens and black poplars whisper and rustle to each other the latest "tales of a far countree," brought to them by the breath of the sea, whose voice one can hear, in the pauses of the stillness, away at the mouth of the valley. Down a gentle grade where the bicycle, with a remnant of her original sin for which now one only loves her the better as being a proof of her individuality, mischievously tries to run away, and has to be gently corrected with the break, which adds another little crunching sound to the many earth-voices that are speaking on all sides; past apple-orchards where the boughs have to be propped up to prevent the extraordinary weight of fruit breaking them down, and whence the pungent, aromatic smell of the apples is almost intoxicating; past long, low farms typical of comfort, prosperity, and neatness, with their great *basses cours*, their *jardins potagers* (where the gigantic sunflowers, eight or ten feet high, have nodded their golden heads and gone to sleep drooping over the heavily-burdened dwarf pear-trees and the bushes of monthly roses that divide the plots of vegetables), and their fertile paddocks carefully enclosed on all sides by high grass banks, on which are planted double and treble rows of beeches and elms in characteristic Norman fashion; past the spinning-mill, where the restless bobbins are at last quiet, and the water-wheel has ceased to turn; and then at last one comes out into the broad valley, with its splendid pasturages, fed by a beautiful little purling trout-stream, whence come those peckled beauties I shall have, "*à la meunière*," at dinner presently. Through the softly-rising, silvery mist the cows loom large as they stand, hoof deep, in the rich grass, lowing "for want of thought," as one after the other passes through the hands of the milkers before being left in the fields for the night.

Over the shoulder of the down, on the left, rises in a golden glory the crescent moon, standing proudly erect, radiant and effulgent and gracious; and to her, Diana, fair huntress of the skies, typical of the beauty of that single blessedness which is the crowning merit of the bicycle, on whose wheels I have run away so far, I offer my humble orisons that she may be gracious to her handmaid and remember her prayer. For would this twilight ride have been the same with a companion? Not a bit of it. A companion would have necessitated speech, the tiresome repetition of words, useless comment; and how contemptible and puerile are the cramping boundaries of spoken words and comments when all Nature is raising her voice in an Evening Hymn, which, to those who are alone with the Great Mother, and who have been taught by her to see, and, above all to hear, rolls and echoes in glorious strophe and antistrophe, right up to the purple vault above our heads, gemmed with the myriads of stars, worlds upon worlds of that never-ending Beauty whose worship is the one pure religion! No! a companion is not always either a thing of beauty or a joy for ever; he or she is often a stopper in a vial of perfume, a discordant note in the otherwise perfect harmony, an ever-present weight. Like trout fishing, bicycling has joys that are unknown to those who seek them not in solitude—

And just when I have reached this point I am suddenly aware of an unpleasant sensation in my hind wheel, a break in the usual smoothness to which I am so much accustomed that only an interruption makes me aware of it. I dismount, knowing pretty well what has happened; the pneumatic tyre has "leaked," and needs being blown out again. And while I prop the machine against the high bank, and taking out the little pump from the wallet hung behind the saddle proceed to inflate the tyre again, I feel inclined to modify my "last remark but one," and to acknowledge secretly that a companion who would do this tiresome pumping for me would not be altogether out of place. However, the thought is but momentary. The tyre is soon hard and resistent once more, and capable of carrying me for far more kilometres than the four or five that yet separate me from the *truites à la meunière* aforesaid. The joy of independence, of being sufficient to one's own completeness (and to that of one's bicycle, *bien entendu!*), comes over me once more as soon as I am in the saddle; and on through the gathering twilight, as the moon vanishes behind the lofty cliff, I speed. *Il mare mi chiama*, as the Venetians say as soon as they are any way inland. The voice of the sea is calling, calling over these flat water-meadows with their marshy exhala-tions—calling to me to come and breathe the purity of her breath, to rest in the sound of her rustling cadences. On a bicycle, to wish and to do in the matter of speed are one; there is no using a whip on a poor tired horse, no protest from one's conscience at urging on a weary fellow creature. And so, on the wings of the wind, as swiftly, as softly, and as silently, Ixiona carries me back to the haven where I would be, by the shores of the unvintaged sea.

Goblin Gold

A crowd of semi-dejected, semi-angry people stand round the closed window of the ticket office when we arrived at the Gare du Nord. We are too busy seeing our bicycles safely into the station to pay much attention to anything till the apples of our eyes are lifted off the cabs, but Gemini No. I, who has been wandering about like an unappropriated blessing in blue serge knicker-bockers, secure in the knowledge that G. No. 2 will see to the security of their tandem, suddenly attracts our attention by exploding like a squib under the nose of an indifferent official, who is galvanised into life by the furious little lady before him: "Pas de train pour Compiègne à dix heures! C'est marqué sur l'Indicateur," says this anything but Heavenly Twin, with a stamp of a small foot and a general ruffling of feathers that would appal the stoutest male heart. No doubt the official quakes in his shoes, but he manages to preserve a semblance of dignity as he shrugs his shoulders and replies, "Sans doute! il y a des mois que tous les indicateurs devraient être brûlés!"

With this somewhat lean expression of sympathy we have to be content as we prepare for nearly an hour's wait, which is the form of early worm that rewards us for our early rising. We have a good many companions in our misfortune, other bikists, male and female, who have also put their faith in the faithless "Indicateur," and who are also intent on a day in the country. We are once more struck by the difference between the attitude of the various railway administrations towards bicycles and their riders in France and in England. The French railway authorities are wise enough to conciliate and encourage bikists in every possible way. No matter what the distance one may go on all the lines around Paris, whether as far as Calais or as near as Fontainebleau, the only charge for the bicycle being carried in the guard's van is one penny, which represents the registering fee and ticket. What is the result? That every day riders put their machines on the trains and run out of town, to Marly, to Fontainebleau, to St. Germain, to Rambouillet, and heaven knows where besides; while on Sundays and fête-days the riders swarm at the railway stations, and must make a very considerable difference in the traffic returns of the different lines. But in England many of the lines charge ridiculous rates for carrying bicycles, and instead of encouraging people to use the railway to get to Burnham Beeches, to Windsor and Ascot, to Godalming, to the New Forest, and all the many lovely places where a day's ride would be a delight, they do rather the reverse; and for fifty or a hundred riders who use the railways constantly in France, there is hardly one in England.

Our probation of patience comes at last at an end, and we pay our pennies for the tandem as well as Bike and Biquette, over which the porters exchange admiring glances and remarks among themselves as to the peculiarities of the build of the latter with the air of practical experts, which, no doubt, they are. As it is time for *déjeûner* when we get to Compiègne, we hoist the bikes on the omnibus of the Hôtel de la Cloche, and congratulate ourselves on having done so as we are jolted uphill over horribly paved streets till we reach the market-place adorned with a beautiful little Hôtel de Ville and a statue of Jeanne d'Arc with the inscription, "Je yray voyr mes bons amys de Compiengne." By the time we have eaten an excellent and inexpensive breakfast we are quite willing to subscribe to the wisdom of La Pucelle, and we hope the "bons amys" of her day treated her as well as their descendants have treated us. But the day is slipping away, and the gleams of sunlight are becoming more fitful. There have already been several small showers, so if we intend to reach Pierrefonds it behoves us not to linger over our coffee. The paving of the streets suggests anything but a pleasant start, so we walk the bikes up to the château, standing silent and shuttered, dreaming of its past Imperial glories, and then turning sharp to the right are soon in the saddle and speeding along the Avenue Thiers, one of the roads leading into the forest.

At first the roads are deep mire, and even with the best inflated pneumatics the work is hard; but presently we mount a long hill and find ourselves really in the woods, where the rain has not yet penetrated so much, and where the going consequently is much better. Just before reaching the Carrefour Royal, where six or seven roads meet, we come upon a band of youthful seminarists out for a melancholy walk two by two; and their general expression of concentrated envy as we sweep by, free as the birds on the wing, leaves one with an intense feeling of pity, which is accentuated as we pass on into the heart of the woods, where everything speaks of the sanctity of freedom and communion with the Great Mother.

And how glorious the woods are in their autumn beauty! The leaves that lie thickly on the ground are like an Oriental carpet, deep purple, crimson, and orange mingling with the late green of bracken fronds which, under the shelter of the trees, have not yet turned to the copper and bronze that is theirs in the open spaces. Here and there a thread of shining amethyst marks a little path, glistening with wet, winding its way among the boles out of sight, like some shy woodland creature alarmed by the sight of strangers on the road. Overhead is a canopy of gold such as no emperor could rival—gold that fills the very air with radiance like that of the sun itself, and laughs defiance at the grey skies above; goblin gold that flutters down upon us as we pass, making us laugh, like Danaë, with joy at this manifestation of the favour of the woodland gods. The ground rises at either side, and the woodland paths to right and left are like the aisles in some great temple, the branches meeting overhead in a Gothic arch, and the vistas closed in with a glory of colour, of crimson, gold, and green, which can only be likened to a mediaeval stained-glass window through which the sun is shining. The blood-red of the beech, the green of the oaks, the orange-yellow of the horse-chestnuts, mingle with the dark indigo of the pines and the delicate pale gold of the birch-leaves, shining like freshly minted coin above the fragile stems, with their fanciful livery of black and white that recalls the beauty of an ancient *niello*. The loveliness of the woodland sinks into our hearts and laps them in a silence that is the highest appreciation of all great and perfect beauty. Never have I seen any autumn woodland to compare with this Forest of Compiègne, through which we ride as through an enchanted forest in a fairy-tale.

But the compilers of fairy-tales have forgotten to give us details about the state of the roads in their enchanted forests. Those we are riding over are at times like glass, and we are all of us watching who shall experience the first "side slip." The Expert, wishing to note whether his gear-chain is all right, walks a little distance, and can hardly keep his feet at all on the slippery surface. With relief he finds himself once more in the saddle, and, catching us up, is explaining the matter to me, when, as the words "These tyres really seem to hold better on this road than shoes" leave his lips, the demon that invariably lurks in a bike seizes the opportunity. Before he can enunciate the word "shoes" the wheels slip as if mowed down by a scythe, and I have just time to spurt violently ahead to avoid being bowled over by his downfall. I grieve to say that the Gemini and I are so shaking with laughter at the psychological moment chosen for the mishap that we can only just make friendly inquiry over our shoulders. But the Expert's legs are long, and he is active as a cat, so that we are not altogether surprised when he overtakes us, not plastered all down one side with mud, as might have been expected, but clean and unbruised. In fact, he is cleaner than I; for I regret to have to state that Biquette, the adorable machine built especially for me, whose curves are as great a joy to the eye as are her colours of dark blue and silver, whose paces in comparison to those of the ordinary bike are as different as are a thoroughbred's to an ordinary bone-shaking hack—this exquisitely dainty combination of strength and beauty disgraces herself by a most plebeian love of puddles. It is the last stronghold of the demon that inhabits all bikes, for bikes are never altogether tamed. I have cured her of a love of stone-heaps, of side-walks, of drays, and hay-waggons, with all of which, at one time, she imperilled her life and mine; I have taught her to like to go uphill to a certain extent, and not to bolt immoderately at a descent; but to her unregenerate affection for the puddles of the highway she holds with the firmness of a small boy, and with the result that my shoes and stockings present a more than speckled appearance after a mile on a muddy road, for she never misses skimming through a puddle whenever she can.

With a view to letting the Expert see if one of his pedals has been twisted by his fall we call a halt. The tandem and Biquette are propped against a bank while Bike is being overhauled, and the sub-heavenly Twins and I squabble as to who shall sit on the milestone. They, being two to one, as well as small and determined, gain the day, and I am reduced to perching on a pile of wood which has been stacked by the wood-cutters, whose little huts we have seen through the trees from time to time. The sound of a horn comes to us through the golden silence, accompanied by that of a pair of horses trotting with a carriage. Looking up the long vista we see shy rabbits lopping across the road and pheasants scuttling down one bank and over to the wood at the other side. The sound of the horn comes ever nearer, and presently a line of beaters in long yellow canvas blouses, accompanied by some *gardes-de-chasse*, appear through the wood, and, crossing the bank, call a halt in the road. Some of the men are carrying game, and the one nearest to us throws down on the road, with an "ouf!" of relief, a dead roebuck. Ah, the pity of it!

to see that lovely little creature with its bleeding head, glazed eyes, and stiffening limbs, and to think that only a short time ago it was joying in its free life in these glorious woods, making the face of Nature more complete and beautiful with its own beauty. In spite of being probably accused of sentimentality, I confess it makes me sick with pity to see the lovely dead thing lying in the muddy road, and I am heartily glad when at another blast on the horn the beaters and keepers gather themselves and their game together and disappear into the wood over the opposite bank of the road.

The sound of the horn dies away, but that of the trotting horses continues, sometimes so near that we look down the road to see the carriage, sometimes almost dying away in the distance. It becomes distinctly eerie after a time, and all the more so when a real material vehicle with one horse creeps up silently over the leaves behind us and makes its soundless way through the wood, while the hoofs of the unseen horses ring out clear through the stillness. I can see that something of unconfessed fear is creeping over the Twins, and they jump to their feet with delight when the Expert, having tinkered all Bike's screws with the spanner, announces he is ready to start. In the all-diffused golden radiance we do not notice the grey-sodden clouds that have crept up overhead. The goblin gold fills our eyes to the exclusion of everything but the woodland, which becomes more beautiful every moment, the trees widening out and growing larger and more stately in their individual beauty, while the bracken rolls its bronze and copper down the open slopes.

> "Then up with your heads, ye sylvan lords,
>   Wave proudly in the breeze;
> From our cradle-bands to our coffin-boards
>   We're in debt to the forest trees."

I am interrupted in my enthusiastic quotation by a rain-drop of large size in one eye, and the voice of the Expert in my ear. "I don't know much about cradle-bands," he remarks grimly, "but I think coffin-boards will be in request if we don't get to Pierrefonds before the rain soaks us to the skin." He speaks only too truly as regards the rain. Down it comes, and sends us flying along at top speed, thankful that we are on bicycles and dependent on our own exertions and not on those of a quadruped. Furious riding it is, for in this weather all hope of visiting the Château de Pierrefonds, Viollet-le-Duc's masterpiece of mediaeval restoration, must be abandoned, and we have barely time to catch the train to take us back to Paris. I nearly demolish an ancient gentleman, and the Twins on the tandem send three children into hysterics. But these are minor details in a race against rain and time, and we arrive at the station with a minute to spare to rub down the faithful bikes before putting them into the train. And panting, rosy, happy with our ride and triumphant with its termination, we glide in the train out of the quiet little valley, promising ourselves to return at some future moment and visit the magnificent donjon that frowns on us from its overhanging rock through the grey curtain of rain.

The Temple of Mammon

It is curious how small a thing will often start one off to do something that one has long desired to do, but which would probably remain undone without a special incentive. The immediate cause of my finding myself on Tower Hill was not a desire to attend a meeting of the unemployed, or to listen to the impassioned utterances of a Socialist orator setting forth the attractive gospel of plundering one's neighbours, but the fact that, having received one of the new sovereigns in some change, I felt it was incumbent on me to see how the new coins were made with the least possible delay. Tower Hill was deserted when we got there; neither employed nor unemployed were visible as we drifted on past the garden which edges the moat of the Tower, where the lilac bushes are putting out their tender green leaves tentatively, as if fearful of being nipped by the frosts that garnish an English spring. The Tower looks more like a large toy out of Cremer's shop than ever, owing to the presence of some little red toy soldiers on the ramparts, no doubt put there by the authorities as attractive samples to back up the advertisement for soldiers and sailors that hang on the rails of the garden. "Smart active lads wanted" is the legend being diligently scanned by a poor tatterdemalion with lank hair, rounded shoulders, and hollow cheeks; he cannot be said to answer to the description of the desired article—but great is the power of discipline, and perhaps he may turn out better than he looks.

As we move away from him the Temple of Mammon looms imposingly at the other side of the road, behind a set of double railings separated by a moat. There are two entrances. Needless to say, being human, we make our way to the wrong one, and are extracted from our dilemma by the sentry arriving, no doubt to see what we are doing trying to force an entrance at the wrong door. We debate whether we shall address him, for vague ideas that "one should not speak to the man at the wheel" also applies to sentries, deter my nervous companion. However, as he approaches, and we discover that this is no bearded warrior, but a callow fledgeling who probably knows more about pop-guns than Enfields, we demand and receive the information we require, which he supplements by following closely on our heels till he has seen us into the doorway. A policeman guards the gate; he seems much alarmed at our approach, and claps the gate to until he has heard the "open-sesame" of the Governor's name. Bolts and bars are then thrown back, and we find ourselves in the great courtyard, inside the moat of jet-black water wherein a solitary goldfish, no doubt worn out by the effort of competing with all the gold in his immediate neighbourhood, has given up the ghost and left his poor little earthly tenement, floating wrong side uppermost in the inky water.

Across a penitential pavement of cobblestones we make our way to the Palace of the King of the Universe—*en passant*, it may be noticed that he is considerably better lodged than his brother sovereign at Buckingham Palace. Beside the stately proportions of the Mint, Buckingham Palace would look more like a county lunatic asylum than ever. A flower-bed in the centre of the court is ablaze with the gold of crocuses, and evidently the official mind disregards the proverb that "all is not gold that glitters," for the glittering crocuses are as carefully enclosed in a covering of wire as if they were freshly-minted sovereigns. The Governor and two other officials join us as soon as we arrive, and being, as usual, late—it is never well to break a recognised habit, good or bad, as it confuses one's identity in the minds of one's friends—we are hurried off at once on the tour of inspection, which begins, as it should, at the beginning of all things—the melting-room.

We are in luck, for we have happened to arrive on a gold day, and in the melting-room devoted to the precious metal the men are hard at work pouring the beautiful orange-and-flame-coloured liquid into rows of upright moulds, which form the gold into bars. The pots or crucibles, made of a mixture of plumbago and earth,

Gold-Melting

are filled with the gold in ingots and with the required amount of alloy, and covered over with charcoal to prevent the gold from being discoloured; and as two workmen, armed with iron hooks, pour the metal into the moulds, another holds a gas-jet to the lip of the crucible, so that the gold, being poured through the flame, is kept clean and bright. It looks horribly dangerous work, but it appears that there has only been one accident since 1851, when the Mint was established on its present lines. On that occasion the unfortunate workman upset a pot of molten gold over his leg. Molten gold has a peculiarity, it does not run off a surface like scalding water—it burns in. The man was taken to the hospital, and the gold removed out of his leg and *sent back to the Mint!* Had I been the sufferer I should certainly have felt that to deprive me of the gold which had made itself literally part of myself was adding insult to injury; but no doubt the workman in question considered that the pension he received was preferable to the lumps of gold dug out of his leg.

From the melting-room we pass on to the rolling-room, where the bars of gold are passed through rollers until they are squeezed out into long laths, exactly like the metal ones that support the spring mattress of a bed. I wonder that no millionaire has had the luminous idea of using golden laths for his couch; it is one that should appeal to Sir Gorgius Midas's refined taste! These laths are then tested in a slit to see if they are of the right thickness, and that test not being sufficient for the precision of the Mint, three pieces the size of a sovereign are punched in the middle of each lath and weighed. If the lath passes the second test, it goes on its journey to the draw-bench in another room; if the punched-out pieces are incorrect, the lath or "fillet" returns to the melting-room. At the draw-bench the laths are seized in the jaws of "the dog," an evil-looking monster of iron, who grips the gold bar with his jaws and the links of the chain he is placed on with his tail, the result being that the laths are drawn through two steel rollers slowly with enormous pressure and weight, and all inequalities of thickness reduced to the required evenness. Then come the punching-machines, which punch out "blanks," as the unstamped sovereigns are termed, with amazing quickness, leaving nothing of the lath of metal but a network, which is broken up into bundles and goes back to the melting-pot. After the punching, the little metal discs, looking exactly like buttons, are shot through another machine, which clips each disc at either side on its passage, giving that raised, protecting edge which preserves the design from wear in its course through the world. These last three processes, the drawing, punching, and edging, all take place in the same room; so it is some time before another door needs to be unlocked for us to go into the annealing room, where the blanks are packed into pots covered with charcoal and softened in furnaces. Out of this kitchen-like place opens appropriately what bears a strong resemblance to a scullery. The air is full of the vapour of boiling water, for here the silver coins, which get discoloured by their various baptisms of fire, undergo baths of sulphuric acid, which, it appears, is "matchless for the complexion" of silver coins. After the sulphuric acid they are rinsed in cold water, and emerge with all the virgin whiteness of peppermint lozenges, and are then rolled in sawdust and dried over a fire.

Through more locked doors, each door being fastened behind us as we pass through (for no workman is allowed to leave his special room without the permission or the certificate of the officer in charge, and in fact cannot do so, as no workman is allowed a key), we are conducted to the coining-room, the last and crowning process in the coin's career. Eight machines are thundering away, turning out all manner of coins for the benefit of the English race at home and abroad: sovereigns, half-crowns, sixpences, ten-cent bits for Hong Kong, and nickel halfpennies for Jamaica. To watch the machines at work is perfectly delightful; their delicacy and precision are exquisite. The machines are

fed by a shoot in which the piles of blanks are placed;
arrived at the level of the moulds, a claw-shaped piece
of brass takes hold of them one by one, pushes forward
the blank into the required position over one punch and
under the other, and at the same time, with a motion
of its claw-like finger, it knocks the finished coin out
of the way into a downward shoot, from whence it is
spat out in all its brilliant new polish into a basin on the
floor. The Governor takes out his watch and times one
of the machines, much as a physician notes the pulse of
a patient; the machine is coining at the rate of one hundred and forty a minute, and the bowl at the foot is very
soon brimming over with the golden treasure.

Conversation is next door to impossible in that thundering din, but as soon as we are outside in the passage,
on our way to the weighing-room, I ask how is it possible to prevent peculation when such quantities of
precious metal and coin are lying about. The answer
is very simple. The amount of metal given out to each
room every morning is weighed and entered in a ledger;
the men have no communication with anything or anybody outside their particular room, wherein they work
all day in different clothes to those they wear outside;
and before they leave in the evening the metal or coin
is again weighed and every ounce accounted for. Only
once has there been a theft of an ounce of gold, and

that was discovered immediately. The only department where this precision of weighing is not possible is in the melting-room, for some metal, of course, must adhere to the pot as well as to the charcoal which covers the five thousand pounds' worth of gold contained by each crucible every time it is put in the fire.

From the coining-room we are taken on to the weighing-room, where what look like a number of small sewing-machines, each enclosed in a locked glass case, are silently weighing every sovereign that is coined in the Mint. These machines weigh to the hundredth part of a grain, and as each sovereign or half-sovereign takes its place in turn on the balance, it is weighed automatically. If it is too heavy or too light the machine gives it a little contemptuous shove to right or left, which causes it to fall into one of the three slots under the machine, while if it should be the absolutely correct weight it is dropped with silent approval into the centre hole that leads to salvation and currency. It is really hard to believe while one watches these exquisite little machines at work that they are not sentient things aware of what they are doing, so precise and, apparently, intelligent is every movement. It is an additional proof of the extraordinary exactitude of the Mint, that, in spite of all the previous tests as to size and weight that the precious metal undergoes during its transformation into current coin, something between thirty and forty per cent. of the gold coins submitted to the weighing-room are sent back to the melting-pot as either too heavy or too light. In a window sits a lad "ringing" sovereigns on a piece of metal to see if any of them are cracked; the coins fly out from under his fingers in a continuous fountain of gold that gleams in the light like a rainbow, but no matter how fast they fly the lad's practised ear catches at once the dull sound emitted by the damaged coin.

But our time is slipping away fast in the midst of all these wonders of the Temple of Mammon, and so we are hurried downstairs to the treasure-house, the Aladdin's cave where silver and gold ingots are piled in a profusion that makes them seem commonplace and of no account; and it is only when we are informed of the value of a shelf full of yellow bars that look like some new kind of gingerbread, and are told that a trifle of half a million reposes there, that we feel as impressed as we ought to be. From the treasure-house we go across the yard to the die-room, where the designs, after being reduced to the required size by a pantograph, are struck in cones of the hardest steel by a press that gives a blow of thirty tons. Two blows are necessary, and, as may be imagined, the fitting together of the punch and the die before the second blow is given is a matter of the most delicate care.

By the time we have taken a fleeting glance at the Museum, with its beautiful collection of coins of all ages, bequeathed to the Mint by Miss Bankes, and its curiosities of all kinds connected with coining, legal and illegal, we are fairly exhausted by the effort to assimilate so much information. For two hours and a half have we been drinking in facts with eyes as well as ears, and even my thirst for information is well nigh sated. So, limp, but enthusiastic, we make our way past the caged crocuses and the defunct goldfish, out of the portals of the Temple of Mammon, where his satellites are busy all day turning out the one thing in the world that every one needs, and that, by all accounts, no one ever has enough of.

In a Signal-Box

Not very long ago I was at Charing Cross Station, seeing off some friends who were starting for the Continent; and, being somewhat too early, I occupied myself watching, as well as I could, the working of the points and signals by the men in the raised signal-box which spans the bridge across the river. Many things I noticed puzzled me much, as to their working in unison and otherwise; and as I was too busy speeding the parting guests, I determined to prosecute my researches at another moment. Having a spare morning soon after, I posted off to Charing Cross; and, taking my courage in both hands, as the French say, I proceeded to beard the station-master in his den. Here my passing fancy was suddenly changed into a fixed determination by being met with a stern refusal. The station-master declared that my proposed visit to the signal-box was an impossibility; that no one was allowed up there except the officials in charge, and that there was nothing to see, nothing which could possibly interest me. On this latter point I ventured to differ; and the station-master, though relenting in spite of himself, still tried to hold his own by declaring that if I would accompany him along the platform he would soon show me there was nothing to see. Needless to say, I asked nothing better, counting on the enthusiasm to which any one at the head of a big organisation is sure to give way when he finds a really interested and appreciative listener. Nor was I wrong; for no sooner is my guide fairly persuaded that an outsider, a mere unit in that great public he looks upon much as a drover does on a herd of cattle, can really be interested in this special hobby and occupation of his, than he is willing to answer all the questions I pour into his ears.

By the time we have reached the end of the platform, and he has explained to me the working of the

Interior of a Signal-Box

locking-bars at the sides of the rail-points (while I
have expressed my sincere surprise that so admirable
an invention should have evolved from the brain of a
grocer), he has softened so far that, seeing the long-
ing looks I cast at the Promised Land in the shape of
the lofty signal-box away out there over the bridge,
his stern resolves vanish, and, dodging a train or two,
we pick our way across the network of rails, ascend
a precipitous companion ladder, and find ourselves in
mid-air on the signal-bridge. A few more steps upwards
and we are in the glass-house where the two men and a
boy whose watch it is are busy with the destinies of the
trains and engines that ceaselessly pass to and fro below.

Down one side is a range of ninety-seven levers, some red, some black, others green. The red are the signals, the black are the points, and the green the distance signals as to change of roads for incoming trains at the other end of the bridge. The two men work the levers, while the small boy keeps the ledger of the trains. I look on in bewildered amazement as these men walk up and down the long range of levers, pulling them down here and there; it is as if it were some gigantic musical instrument on which they strike the chords that produce the harmony below among those conflicting strings of rails. But this instrument has at least the merit that wrong notes are an impossibility. Every red lever (which governs the signals of any one of the five "roads") has a series of figures painted on it in black; some have only one or two, others have as many as seven or eight. These numbers represent the point-levers which are on the same road, and until all those point-levers are down the signal-lever which governs them cannot be moved. If the signalman forgot a point, and tried to move the red lever, he would find it impossible to do so; but as soon as the points are set correctly the signal-lever can then be put down, and, once down, none of those point-levers can be moved without putting back the signal-lever to "danger." This is what is called the "interlocking" system, and precludes all possibility of accident from either care-lessness or malevolence; for if the signalman is careless he is recalled by the immovable signal-lever, and, should mischief be wilfully intended, it is impossible to carry it out without putting back the signal to "danger." It certainly is a most admirable invention, for in so extraordinarily complex a system accidents would be bound to happen without some such precaution.

Even as it is, it is nothing short of marvellous to stand by and note how the two signalmen have the whole organisation of the train service at their fingers' ends. Trains coming in; trains going out; loose engines careering backwards and forwards; trains waiting on the bridge till a platform is free for them whereat to discharge their passengers; empty lines of carriages being brought up from the depot at the other side of the river, to be broken up into various trains during the course of the day; horse-boxes and carriage-trucks going off to the Waterloo crossing, there to be shunted on to that line; trains arriving from Maidstone, Redhill, or elsewhere, which need to be signalled to (by one of the green levers) at the other end of the bridge which "road" they are to come in by, according to the state of the platforms—all this unceasing brain-work is carried through by the two signalmen on Charing Cross Bridge with a calm precision which is really extraordinary.

Their watch is of eight hours' duration, and I only wonder how they can stand the work even for so long, for the bridge signal-box is one of the most, if not the most, important on the whole line; for here the whole enormous traffic is held, as it were, in one controlling hand, each of the five "roads" representing a finger. There is another signal-box of great importance, I am told, at what is called the "Crossing," the point at the other side of the river where all the traffic from Charing Cross, Cannon Street, and London Bridge Stations converges, and where something like eight hundred trains a day cross in and out of each other's lines! At Charing Cross alone four hundred and seventy trains pass in and out in the twenty hours, for from I A.M. to 5 A.M. the public cease from troubling and the trains can be at rest.

Over the long range of levers a series of indicating discs are placed against the wall between the windows. Some are "train describers," and the large dial bears a number of smaller ones, with the names of various stations. As I look at one an electric bell rings, and the needle swings round to the little dial marked "Cannon Street," the sign that a train has just left there which will reach Charing Cross in about seven minutes. "Ping!" goes another bell, and my eye is caught by a glass-covered box, where one of the red caps that cover

five little holes in a sheet of cardboard has fallen, discovering a number——No. 3——which, being interpreted,
means that the platform inspector has a train ready
to start at No. 3 platform, and thus warns the signalmen "to set the road"; until they have done so, and the
corresponding signal is set, the train cannot start; for
outside the signal-box the only signs the officials know
anything about are the signals. They read the signals,
one and all, and act accordingly, for blind unquestioning
obedience is the first principle inculcated, and rightly
so, in railway discipline. This electric warning from
the platform inspector is the substitute for the frightful
steam whistling which other station authorities indulge
in on the plea of giving notice when the trains are ready
to start; and certainly all travellers by the S.E. line
should feel grateful that this nuisance is abolished at
Charing Cross. A single tiny whistle as the train actu-
ally starts is all that is allowed, and one's tympanum
is spared the ear-splitting shrieks one is afflicted with
on other lines.

In another glass-covered box is a miniature sema-
phore, which works also by electricity between this
signal-box and the next at the other side of the bridge.
It signals that a train is starting, and the other signals
when it has passed and the road is again clear, this all
being part of the "block system" which has done so

much to ensure safety in railway travelling. When I see the amount of work and warning which the passage of every train means, the question of special trains suggests itself, and I turn to the station-master to ask him what does he do when some private individual comes to him and demands a "special" regardless of "special" rates? "Take his money first," answers my guide promptly, with a twinkle in his keen grey eyes; and then explains how a telegraphic warning is sent to every station-master along the whole line that a special is coming through at such an hour, and the line must be clear; for even if the special were sent through at an hour when there were no other trains passing, warning is necessary, lest, for instance, the platelayers should be at work in a tunnel, and have taken up a line, knowing that no regular train was due on it. No wonder people have to pay high for a special train; in fact, it must mean such an immense amount of trouble all along the line that the only surprising thing is that the authorities should consent to run one at any price. When it is decided to make permanent additions to the train service, the station-masters of Charing Cross, Victoria, Cannon Street, and London Bridge meet in solemn conclave at the superintendent's office (like generals on the eve of an engagement), and decide where and when the additional trains can be fitted in.

As an occupation, this sorting of trains must much resemble the *Kriegspiel* in general intricacy and bewilderment as to what will be the final result. As I stand here on the upper bridge, watching the ceaseless *va-et-vient* of the trains and locomotives below, all following each other, and fitting into their several places like the pieces of a Chinese puzzle, with never a hitch or a pause anywhere, and all controlled by that shining line of levers, I am filled with amazement at the organisation and brain-work that all this smoothness means. Underneath the floor on which I stand is the machinery of the levers, each one being controlled by cams; and through the window my guide points out to me the arrangements on the switch-rods to compensate the metal against the atmospheric changes of this pleasing climate. No detail seems to have been forgotten, no precaution neglected: and as, after leaving the signal-box, I pause for a moment, looking out over the great cantilever bridge and its restless traffic down to the river below, shining like molten silver in the morning sunlight, where long lines of barges are being towed up-stream by hard-working little tugs, I feel that it is good to be here, and to put one's finger, as it were, for a moment on one of the main arteries of this most complex of cities, the Modern Babylon.

Billingsgate

I found myself one day with a party of friends mounting the steps of the Monument Station in the City, and descending that steep but ornamental thoroughfare, Pudding Lane, famous in civic history as the place where ended the Great Fire that had devastated the City from Pie Corner, near St. Paul's. Turning to the left, we have ocular proof that history is not more accurate than usual, for some way further on we come to the Cock Tavern, where, conspicuous under a glass case at the entrance, are the charred remains of the sign of the original tavern, on the same site, which suffered destruction in the Fire of 1666. A large building alongside announces itself as being the "Billingsgate Christian Mission," and no doubt the Billingsgate Christians from the market opposite are all the better for its ministrations. However, as we came to see the market, not the mission, we do not linger long in the odour of sanctity; but, having grappled with the odour of fish instead, we pass in between the great iron gates, and find ourselves in what I think I can truthfully state to be the very dirtiest place I have ever been in. The market has been late, and is only just over, so there has been no time yet to turn on the powerful hose wherewith the place is washed out every day. The floor is several inches thick in liquid mud and fish-scales and general refuse; but after having come so far, we are not to be daunted by either a Slough of Despond or of Slime. I hear one of the party mutter consolingly something about the advantage of seeing a place in its *couleur locale*; and, encouraged by this right-minded way of viewing the situation, we follow Leezie Lindsay's example, and, "kilting our coats," regardless of onlookers, step gallantly into the slush. To any one of my sex who feels inclined to follow my example and visit Billingsgate Market when it is in full blast, I would recommend the use of Louis XV. heels—the higher the better—in fact, a pair of stilts would not be inappropriate. On all sides are fish great and small, or at least what is left of them now that the chief sales are over; and an ancient and a fish-like smell of considerable penetrating force hangs around us fondly. Well may we exclaim with Mercutio, "O flesh, flesh, how art thou fishified!" for I am haunted by a notion that it will take all the perfumes of Araby to counteract the effect of the *bouquet de merlans* and the *triple extrait de soles* which we seem to be absorbing at every pore. On one counter we find laid out four huge, flat, oval fish, with which we are not acquainted by sight. We are told they are halibut, which, when fried in oil and served cold, form one of the most popular dishes among the Jews.

One of the largest fish merchants of the place takes us in hand, and gives us no end of interesting information about the famous market, which is under the control of the Corporation. The present building has only been built about twenty-six years, and a fine spacious one it is, hung with a profusion of shaded gas-lamps, which, it can be imagined, are pretty necessary in a place where the business hours are generally from three in the morning to ten or twelve o'clock midday. We inquire with affectionate interest about the proverbial force and picturesque variety of the Billingsgate language, and are much disappointed to hear that it is decreasing in power. No doubt it will soon degenerate to the level of Tommy Atkins's "six hundred nouns and *one adjective*." Evidently the Billingsgate Mission has much to answer for. It is to be hoped that the degeneration in strength of language will not be followed by degeneration of strength of body, for the Billingsgate porters are as stalwart a lot of men as one could wish to see; and our guide says he would back them to carry weight against any other set of men in London. He recounts with pardonable pride how he took one of his porters down to Grimsby once, and how the fishermen looked with disdain on the "chap from Lunnon," until the aforesaid "chap" dumfounded them all by carrying *four hundredweight* in a fish-box or "trunk" on his head for a distance of 120 yards, and then tossed his load down on to the shore, where it remained as a monument and a warning to the scoffers. To enable them to carry these great weights on their heads, the Billingsgate porters wear curious square pads inside a sort of skull-cap of leather, which fits over the head. It appears that the muscles most developed by this sensible way of carrying burdens are those of the neck and of the calves of the legs; and it certainly gives an uprightness of carriage very different from the usual slouching gait of porters in other trades.

Through the slush and slime we go as best we may, and ascend the stairs that lead up to the famous Three Tuns, the "fish ordinary" of Billingsgate, where we are to lunch. We are taken into a large bright room, with a long line of windows overlooking the river. Our table is placed in the far corner, where there is an end window looking over the Custom House quay and down the river to the Tower Bridge. The view both ways is full of variety, owing to the passing barges and steamers. The tide is coming in, and the barges are floating up with that delightful indifference to getting in other people's way which makes their presence so much appreciated on the Thames. Just in front of our window are three curious-looking lighters, unusually bluff in the bows, and adorned with great wooden fins along their sides (the said fins being used to hold the water and allow greater pressure of sails being used). These are the Dutch eel-schuyts, which bring over live eels to the London market. The eels are enclosed in a curious sort of cage under the centre of the vessel, through which the sea passes at will—an excellent method of transport until Gravesend is reached. There, however, the water of the Thames becomes so poisonous that if the eels were left therein under the vessel they would yield up the ghost (considering the extreme tenacity of life in an eel, this fact speaks volumes for Thames water!); so at Gravesend they are scooped up out of the cage and put in boxes on the deck until they arrive at Billingsgate. These Dutch schuyts pay no tollage of any kind to the Port of London, free anchorage having been granted to three Dutch eel-boats by Queen Elizabeth, the only condition attaching to the privilege being that there must always be three vessels at anchor in front of Billingsgate Wharf. If one were to go away before another arrived to take its place, the privilege would be lost, and tollage claimed.

As we sit listening to these and other details of the fish trade, we are busily employed not only eating fish, but breathing it too. The fish we eat is certainly better than the fish we breathe; it is not only presented in a pleasanter form to our senses, but it is also indubitably more juvenile. I should say that the fish in the air dated from Noah, while the fish on our plates must have been alive yesterday. Excellent as it is, however, there are limits to the amount one can swallow; five or six courses of fish, followed by roast lamb, are too large a contract for us, and we can only sigh in astonishment that such a meal, *plus* vegetables, bread, and cheese *ad lib.*, can be supplied at two shillings a head. We are waited on by a lean and skinny cat, who turns up a very smutty nose at the fish we offer; she probably sighs for birds, and thinks of a mouse as we do of an ortolan. Such is the *ewiges Sehnen und Streben* of existence, whether human or feline! When we feel that we shall not be able to look a fish in the face again for many a day to come, and have devoured strawberries and cream, and sampled the famous Billingsgate punch (which certainly deserves to be classed amongst meritorious beverages), we tear ourselves away from our sunny corner. Leaning out of the window, we see below the barges ranged alongside the quay, full of "returned empties," the open fish "trunks" in which the fish is brought from Grimsby every day. A row of men and boys are sitting on the quay and about the barges, resting after their labours, while some urchins are mudlarking in a way which deserves being chronicled by the brush of Tom Browne or Raven Hill. At the opposite side of the river a steamer is unloading straw and hay at Chamberlain's Wharf, the buildings that open into Tooley Street, where the famous fire took place some forty years ago. Out of the dock alongside the burning ship was towed on that memorable occasion, when some one had succeeded in "setting the Thames on fire."

We leave the room, and pause in the gallery, which looks into the market itself. From this coign of vantage we get an insight into the various processes of what is technically known as "faking" the inferior residue of the fish, which ultimately finds its way to Whitechapel and similar districts, where it helps to raise the well-known perfume of those fragrant neighbourhoods. Two lads are busy packing a lot of soles which are no longer in the first blush of youth, only in their case old age and its drawbacks are arrested by cramming the gills of each fish full of ice; other fish—gurnards, gray mullet, haddocks, &c.—are being scraped, trimmed, and cut up into slices, which act as a most effectual disguise of the original creature's appearance and peculiarities. I look in vain for sturgeons, which sometimes arrive at Billingsgate, great monsters sixteen feet long; but there are none on view to-day. We descend by another staircase from that by which we ascended, and are shown the lift which conveys to the basement the cases of lobsters and crabs; for in the basement are the vast cauldrons where these crustacea are boiled. The popular Billingsgate superstition will have it that the lobsters utter a sound, an ejaculation, which, if learnt during their short sojourn in the market, is likely to be something more vigorous than "How hot!" when they are immersed; but I somehow disbelieve these tales of the "swan-song" of the lobster. They are packed in circular cases, all with their claws securely tied, and in these cases they are boiled, which, considering the hundreds that go into the cauldrons together, is a much more expeditious method than having to extract them singly afterwards.

As we are standing looking down into this pit of darkness, the lobster's Inferno, a man passes us in a kind of uniform. We learn that he is a "condemner," a sort of Billingsgate High Inquisitor, whose business it is to go on board every steamer and fish-boat that arrives at Billingsgate Wharf, and to examine every "trunk" of fish to see whether it is fit for food. I gaze respectfully at his nose, for verily it must be an heroic organ to go through such a daily ordeal of sniffing! He tells us, with a gleam of perfectly justifiable pride, that he and his brother "condemners" have condemned two hundred and ninety trunks out of the seven thousand received at Billingsgate that morning. I shiver at the thought of two hundred and ninety sniffs at decaying fish, and I think that if the V.C. were hung at the tip of that heroic proboscis, it would not be too great a reward; for, after all, what is the "imminent deadly breach" to a turbot that has seen better days?

The market is being cleared for its daily toilette, and we stand aside while we watch the hose beginning its much-needed labours—for only a rushing stream of water can cope with such an accumulation of slime and mud—but presently the hose begins to "box the compass" in our direction, and we think it wisest to take refuge in flight.

A Suburban Gallery

If "misery," as it is said, "makes strange bedfellows," a certain form of it—illness—often conduces to strange reading; and during a six weeks' Armageddon with the fiends of neuralgic rheumatism, I have had time to turn up all sorts of out-of-the-way and forgotten volumes, which, as a rule, in these days of express speed, one never has time to read. Among others, I came across Leigh Hunt's "Essays," and happening upon his walk from Dulwich, it revived in me a long-dormant desire, which had first come upon me years ago when I read "Alton Locke," to visit the Gallery there. The mere fact of being physically incapable of walking across the room made the desire considerably more vivid; and when my doctor remonstrated, I annihilated him with Leigh Hunt's words, "Illness, you know, does not hinder me from walking, neither does anxiety. On the contrary, the more I walk, the better and stouter I become; and I believe if everybody were to regard the restlessness which anxiety creates as a signal from Nature to get up and contend with it in that manner, people would find the benefit of it." Esculapius replied, that if I thought Leigh Hunt a better doctor than he, there was nothing more to be said, and thereupon took both his hat and his departure; while I "got up and contended" in the manner prescribed, and with the aid of two sticks and a bodyguard found myself at Victoria Station.

But to find oneself at Victoria Station is a much easier matter than to find a booking-office where the powers that be will, of their charity, condescend to give you a ticket for Dulwich in exchange for filthy lucre. My humble demand is treated with scorn at four *guichets*. Human nature, especially when racked with rheumatism, is frail; and on turning away from office No. 4 my pent-up feelings find vent in a forcible monosyllable, which has a most wonderful effect on a dejected little woman who is apparently in the same boat with me. She flushes a bright pink, and looks at me with such evident gratitude that I am almost tempted to give her the vicarious pleasure a second time; but this is clearly not the spirit with which to rise from a bed of sickness, so I hobble off, and by throwing myself on the mercy of the clerk of the Continental ticket office, at last secure the coveted bits of pasteboard and make my way to the very end of the interminable platform, where, as usual, the company elects to leave its trains, with a thoughtful desire to make the passengers walk as far as they can. Before I get there, I am already beginning to doubt Leigh Hunt's wisdom in saying, "The more I walk, the better and stouter I become;" but, to quote another ancient, "Everything in this world comes to an end except Harley Street," and even Victorian platforms are no exception to this rule.

Once we have captured the tickets and the train, the rest is easy. It does not take long to steam away above the hideousness of Southern London, and its terrible backyards, homes of every untidiness and dirt which it is possible to conceive. General Booth's plan for the regeneration of the Submerged Tenth by means of empty sardine tins must have been revealed to him from a study of London backyards, where those relics of feasting seem to grow luxuriantly. By the comparative study of backyards one can learn the class of neighbourhood one is passing over. Gradually the yards begin to grow something more verdant than clothes-props, or, to put it more poetically, the clothes-props bring forth green leaves like St. Christopher's staff, though they still continue to support lines of fluttering inflated garments. Then gravel-walks appear, and grass plats take the place of mildewy moss; by degrees the clothes-lines, stubborn as they are, vanish, and sunflowers, dahlias, and stucco dogs, "regardant" as they say in heraldry, denote that we have reached the villadom that respects itself, and is sniffingly thankful it is not as other neighbourhoods are. From that stage we pass out into the sweet green fields of the country, so welcome to eyes that have gazed at nothing but bricks and wall-papers for months, and finally pull up at Dulwich, embosomed in trees.

Here we get out, and after negotiating, with a certain amount of difficulty, the remarkably steep staircase that brings us down to the natural level of Mother Earth once more, we hold a council of war on the pavement. We are strangers in the land, and know not how far off the Gallery may be, so we fall victims to the wiles of a cabman, who drives us with much solemnity about a hundred yards round the corner, and deposits us at the gateway of the garden that surrounds the Gallery. If many guileless strangers visit Dulwich, the post of station flyman must be a fairly lucrative one. But I am in such a condition of beaming content at having escaped out of prison, at seeing the sunshine (one never *feels* it in this foggy land!), and feeling the breeze, that nothing can ruffle my happiness. In fact, it is only a stern sense of duty to a preconceived idea that induces me to go into the Gallery at all; I would sooner remain outside watching the clouds racing up from the sea across the blue sky; but I have come to see the Dulwich Gallery, and such errands are not to be trifled with.

In we go, and purchase catalogues wildly; it would have been more conducive to our ultimate salvation and a satisfactory addition of that long account which the Recording Angel, aided by the late Mr. Babbage, will have to "tot up " on Judgment Day, if we had done nothing of the kind; for a more maddening, soul-destroying publication than the catalogue of the Dulwich Gallery, it would be quite impossible to find. It is large and loquacious, giving most excellent biographies of each painter, but it is constructed on the alphabetical principle, which may be extremely convenient to the officials of a gallery, but which simply means madness to the visitor, and makes it perfectly impossible for him or her to carry away any clear and definite remembrance of the pictures. One's mind is on the stretch of trying to remember whether L comes after E or before R, and immediately after that knotty point is

solved, one is plunged into a horrible vortex of whirl-
ing characters, out of which one vainly looks for an
M in the place of a B, and a D in lieu of a Q; and how
is it possible, I ask, to concentrate one's mind on the
lofty questions of Art? "That way madness lies;" and
Juliet, if she had been acquainted with the Dulwich
catalogue, would not have pictured herself playing with
her forefathers' bones, but rather with the letters of the
alphabet. There is no vanity or false pride about me as
regards my knowledge of the alphabet. I look upon it
as a quagmire of difficulties—a bristling porcupine of
fretful distractions. I am not fond of the multiplication
table, but it's "a little 'oliday" in comparison to the
ABC. I never knew but one person who really knew
the relative positions of each letter without having to
run over the alphabet from the beginning, and he was
as near being a congenital idiot as anybody ever was
outside the walls of an asylum; and, therefore, in the
name of the many intelligent victims of that inhuman
foundation-stone of knowledge, I here enter a protest
against alphabetical catalogues.

Before beginning the Dulwich Gallery proper, we
turn to the left into a small room wherein is what is
known as the Cartwright collection, which belonged
to the College long before the Bourgeois bequest of the
Desenfans collection. They are a fairly interesting series

of portraits, of the "tea-tray" order of art mostly. On the left are a number of portraits of the Lovelace family, including a very meek-and-mild version of the famous one of that ilk, "poet and cavalier," and one of the lady whom he addressed as "Anthea" in his poems. If this be the lady "who may command him anything," to judge by her portrait she would not have done amiss to request her faithful poet to provide her with a better *corsetière*. From the Lovelace group we pass on to the Cartwright series, wherein figure the portraits of the donor, William Cartwright (he combined the trades of actor and book-seller, was a son of a contemporary of Alleyne, who built and endowed the old College, and died in 1687), and those of "The first wife of W. Cartwright" and "The last wife of W. Cartwright." How many wives the actor-bookseller had between these first and last ladies we are not told, but one can at least hope that he did not get one resembling "The last Mrs. Cartwright's sister," for a more *rébarbative* dame it would be hard to find. In among the Cartwright series hangs a portrait supposed to be of Queen Elizabeth, and recalling in many ways and details that most interesting series of portraits by Daniel Mytens which were exhibited at the Old Masters at Burlington House some years ago.

On the opposite wall hangs a most cheerful picture, attributed (on what authority is not stated, but it can

hardly be said to be on that of internal evidence) to
Lucas de Heere. It represents a dog-faced man and a
buxom lady joining hands over a skull, while a corpse,
in an open tomb at their feet, surveys the lady with a
supercilious, reproving stare, apparently unconscious
or indifferent to the fact that he has no clothes on,
and is suffering from a double fracture of both patel-
lae. The picture is sprinkled with grim little rhymes
concerning death and the rotting of bones, and other
similarly enlivening subjects; but we are not cheered on
the whole, and turn away into the chief gallery, where
we are soon lost in admiration over the Wouvermans,
William Van de Veldes, and Cuyps, which are enough
in themselves to justify the journey from town. I look
with a sympathetic eye at the portrait of John Philip
Kemble by Beechey, and wonder whether the owner of
that delightful face really suffered from what he per-
sisted in terming his "aitches and pains" as much as I
have done lately. Opposite to him hangs another charming head, that of Thomas Linley (by Gainsborough),
the father of the lovely Mrs. Sheridan. Van Dyck's
beautiful *Portrait of a Knight* (by some attributed to
Rubens) next attracts our eyes, and then we turn in
further delight to the two exquisite Watteaus which
hang opposite, one on each side of the great door that
leads into the mausoleum where lie the bodies of Sir

Peter Francis Bourgeois, the donor of the collection, and
Mr. and Mrs. Noel Desenfans, who left the collection
(made originally for Stanislaus, King of Poland) to Sir
P. F. Bourgeois.

By this time the clock warns us that our hour is
speeding by, and as I have no intention of spending
it all inside four walls, we hurry on past the famous
Murillos, the charming brown-faced *Girl at a Window*
by Rembrandt, the beautiful Velazquez portrait of
Philip IV.—which, though it has suffered from clean-
ing, is still as unapproachable as is everything which
was produced by that greatest giant among painters
since brushes and pigments were invented—and with
a fleeting look at the replica of *Mrs. Siddons as the
Tragic Muse*, and the full-length Gainsborough portraits of Mrs. Moodie and the Linley Sisters, we retrace
our steps through the gallery, and seeing a door open in
the wall on the left, we pass through it, and find ourselves in a delightful garden, a great stretching space
of velvety green turf, with glorious trees. After my
imprisonment, such a place is like a glimpse of paradise.
At one end the garden is enclosed by the walls of the
College itself; but these are almost entirely hidden by
the most magnificent catalpa-tree I have ever seen. It
rises above the roof of the College, its branches sweep
down to the turf on which they rest, and the whole

tree is one great dome of bright green leaves and pyra-
mids of lilac blossoms. The great romping breeze tosses
the leaves and blossoms hither and thither; its play is
somewhat rough, as the petal-strewn turf testifies, but
the catalpa does not seem to mind the rough caresses
of her lover, and bows and curtseys to him in answer.
Two great mulberry-trees seem to appreciate less the
wind's advances; they creak and groan as he rushes
through their branches, and the turf below is sprinkled with their unripe fruit, which look like drops
of blood on the brilliant green. It is suggested that we
should go and look at the College; but I take my stand
under a glorious deciduous cedar, whose brown stem
is wreathed and festooned with purple clematis flowers, and absolutely decline to see any sights but those
before me: the sunlit stretch of turf, with the shadows
of the clouds racing across it; the tossing branches of
the flower-laden catalpa; a white butterfly gleaming
against a dark background of shrubbery; and a blood-
red snapdragon pulsating like a flame in the gloom of
the flower-bed that borders the gravel walk. "Love well
the hour, and let it go" is one of the secrets as to getting
the hidden honey out of life; and it would take more
than an ancient College to drag me away from my day-
dream among the sunshine, the breeze, and the flowers
in Dulwich Garden.

PUSHKIN PRESS—THE LONDON LIBRARY

"FOUND ON THE SHELVES"

THE LONDON LIBRARY (a registered charity) is one of the UK's leading literary institutions and a favourite haunt of authors, researchers and keen readers.

Membership is open to all.

Join at www.londonlibrary.co.uk.

www.pushkinpress.com